The Story
of
Miss Jemima

The Story of
MISS JEMIMA

By
Walter de la Mare

Illustrated by
Nellie H. Farnam

GROSSET & DUNLAP

Publishers   NEW YORK

Published by arrangement with Basil Blackwell, London

Foreword

Childhood has its fancies; and sometimes age believes in childhood's fancies too. Or do you think it was actually there—that fairylike creature in the churchyard seventy-five years ago?

You will have to make up your mind—Walter de la Mare does not say. If you live in brightly lighted streets, among busy crowds of people, you will say "Bosh!" without hesitation. If you live in lonely ways, you may shrug your shoulders and wonder. But if you have imagined the face of a flower nodding to you in the quiet shade, you may be sure, with Susan, that the grandmother is telling only what she really saw.

True it is that some parts of England are famous for their fairies and fairy tales, and perhaps the countryside described here by Walter de la Mare is one.

Or perhaps somewhat the same thing may have happened to him in the little Kentish village where he was born in 1873. He, too, had a lonely and quiet childhood, until he went to St. Paul's Cathedral Choir School in London. Graduating he held a position as a bookkeeper, but in his imagination, all through those eighteen years of uncongenial work, he thought of himself as a poet, and when he was granted a pension by the government, he really became a poet, one of England's most famous writers of modern times.

He has written *Songs of Childhood, Poems, The Return, Peacock Pie, Come Hither* (an anthology of English poetry for "the young of all ages") *On the Edge, the Eighteen Eighties,* and other volumes of poems and stories.

Edith Lowe

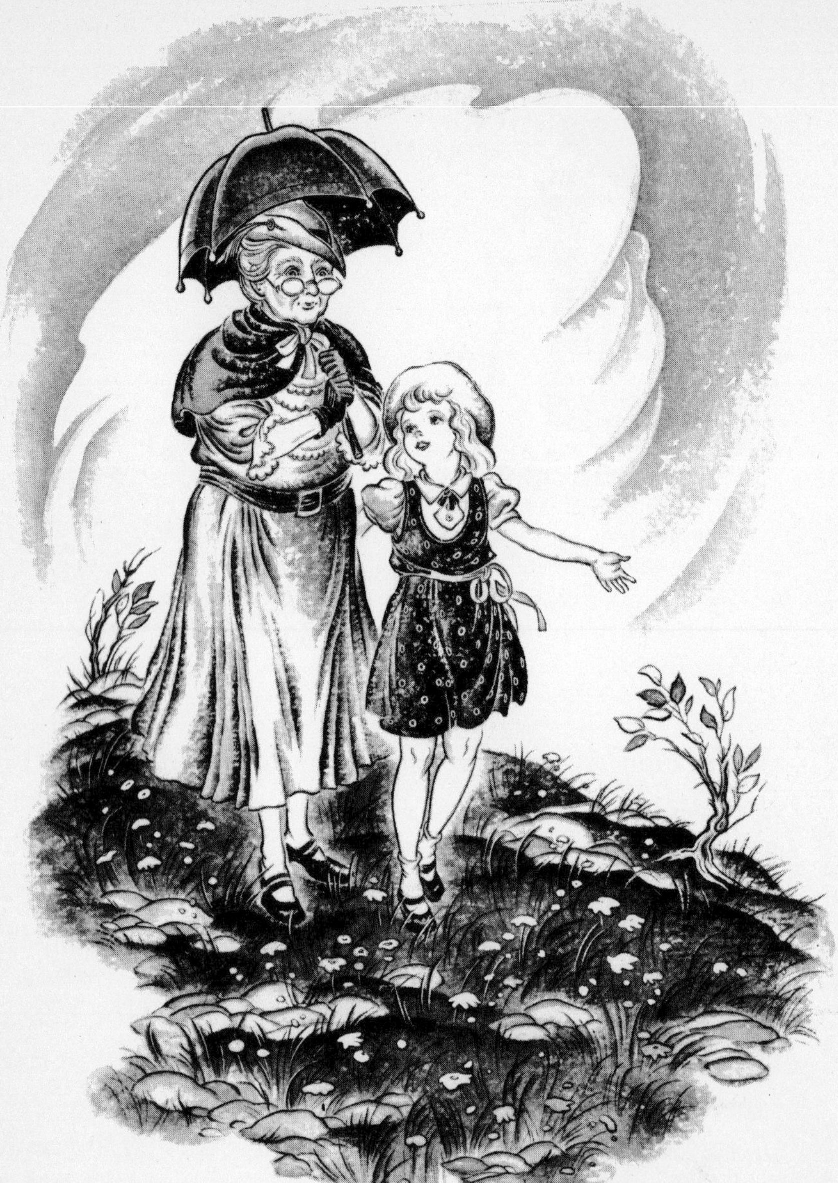

THE STORY OF MISS JEMIMA

It was a hot, still evening; the trees stood motionless; and not a bird was singing under the sky when the little old lady and the child appeared together over the crest of the hill. They paused side by side on the long, green, mounded ridge, behind which the sun was now descending. And spread out flat beneath them were the fields and farms and the wandering stream of the wide countryside. It was quite flat, and a faint thin mist was over it all, stretching out as if to the rim of the world. The little old lady and the child presently ventured a few further paces down the hillside, then again came

to a standstill, and gazed once more, from under the umbrella that shaded them against the hot sun, on the scene
spread out beneath them.

"Is *that* the house, Grannie," said the child, "that one near
the meadow with the horses in it, and the trees? And is that
queer little grey building right in the middle of that green
square field the church?"

The old lady pressed her lips together, and continued to
gaze through her thick glasses at the great solitary country
scene. Then she drew her umbrella down with a click,
placed it on the turf beside her, and sat down on it.

"I don't suppose the grass *is* damp, my dear, after this long
hot day; but you never know," she said.

"It's perfectly dry, Grannie dear, and *very* beautiful," said
the child, as if she could hardly spare the breath for the
words. Then she too sat down. She had rather long fair hair,
and a straight small nose under her round hat with its wreath
of buttercups. Her name was Susan.

"And *is* that the house, Grannie?" she whispered once
more. "And *is* that the church where you did really and
truly see it?"

The old lady never turned her eyes, but continued to over-
look the scene as if she had not heard the small voice
questioning; as if she were alone with her thoughts. And at
that moment, one after another, a troop of gentle-stepping,
half-wild horses appeared on a path round the bluff of the

hill. Shyly eyeing the two strange human figures there in their haunts, one and another of them lifted a narrow lovely head to snort; and a slim young bay, his mane like rough silk in the light, paused to whinny. Then one by one they trotted along the path, and presently were gone. Susan watched them out of sight, then sighed.

"This is a lovely place to be in, Grannie," she said, and sighed again. "I wish I had been here too when I was little. Please do tell me again about the—*you* know."

Her voice trailed off faintly in the still golden air up there on the hill, as if she were now a little timid of repeating the question. She drew in closer beside her grannie, and pushing her small fingers between those of the bent-up, black-gloved hand in the old lady's lap, she stooped forward after another little pause, looked up into the still grey face with its spectacles, and said very softly, *"How* many years ago did you say?"

There was a mild far-away expression in the slate-grey eyes into which Susan was looking, as if memory were retracing one by one the years that had gone. Never had Susan sat like this, upon a green hill, above so immense a world, or in so hushed an evening quiet. Her busy eyes turned once more to look first in the direction in which the trotting comely horses had vanished, then down again to the farmhouse with its barns and byres and orchard. They then rested once more on the grey stone church—which from this height

looked almost as small as a doll's church—in the midst of its green field.

"*How* many years ago, Grannie?" repeated Susan.

"More than I scarcely dare think of," said the old woman at last, gently pressing her fingers. "Seventy-five, my dear."

"Seventy-five!" breathed Susan. "But that's not so very many, Grannie dear," she added quickly, pushing her head against her grannie's black-caped shoulder. "And now, before it is too late, please will you tell me the story. You see, Grannie, soon we shall have to be going back to the cab, or the man will suppose we are not coming back at all. *Please.*"

"But you know most of it already."

"Only in pieces, Grannie; and besides, to think that here we are—here, in the very place!"

"Well," began the old voice at last, "I will tell it to you all again, if you persist, my dear; but it's a little *more* than seventy-five years ago, for—though you would not believe it of such an old person—I was born in May. My mother, your great-grandmother, was young then, and in very delicate health after my father's death. Her doctor had said she must go on a long sea voyage. And since she was not able to take me with her, I was sent to that little farmhouse down there—Green's Farm, as it was called—to spend the months of her absence with my Uncle James and his house-keeper, who was called Miss Jemima."

"Miss Jemima!" cried the little girl, stooping over suddenly with a burst of laughter. "It *is* a queer name, you know, Grannie."

"It is," said the old lady. "And it belonged to one to whom it was my duty to show affection, but who never much cared for the little girl she had in her charge. And when people don't care for you, it is sometimes a little difficult, Susan, to care for them. At least *I* found it so. I don't mean that Miss Jemima was unkind to me, only that when she was kind, she seemed to be kind on purpose. And when I had a slice of plum cake, her face always seemed to tell me it was *plum* cake, and that I deserved only plain. My Uncle James knew that his housekeeper did not think me a pleasant little girl. I was a shrimp in size, with straight black hair, which she made me tie in a pigtail with a piece of velvet ribbon. I had little dark eyes and very skimpy legs. And though he himself was very fond of me, he showed his affection only when we were alone together, and not when she was present. He was ill, too, then, though I did not know *how* ill. And he lay all day in a long chair with a check rug over his legs, and Miss Jemima had charge not only of me, but of the farm."

"*All* the milking, and the ploughing, and the chickens, and the pigs, Grannie?" asked Susan.

The old lady shut her eyes an instant, pressed her lips together and said, "All."

"The consequence was," she went on, "I was rather a solitary child. Whenever I could, I used to hide myself away in some corner of the house—and a beautiful house it is. It's a pity, my dear, I am so old and you so young and this hill so steep. Otherwise we could go down and—well, never mind. That row of small lattice windows which you can see belong to a narrow corridor; and the rooms out of it, rambling one into the other, were walled in just as the builders fancied, when they made the house three hundred years or more ago. And that was in the reign of Edward VI."

"Like the Bluecoat boys," said Susan, "though I can't say I like the yellow stockings, Grannie, not that *mustard* yellow, you know."

"Like the Bluecoat boys," repeated her grandmother. "Well, the house was simply a nest of hiding-places; and I was small—smaller even than you. I would sit with my book; or watch out of a window, *lean* out too sometimes— as if to see my mother in India. And whenever the weather was fine, and sometimes when it was not, I would creep out of the house and run away down that shaggy lane to the little wood you see there. There is a brook in it (though you can't see that) which brawls with a hundred tongues. And sometimes I would climb up this very hill. And sometimes I would creep across the field to that little church.

"It was there I most easily forgot myself and my small scrapes and troubles—with the leaves and the birds, and the blue sky and the clouds overhead, or watching a snail, or picking kingcups and cowslips, or staring into the stream at the fish. You see I was rather a doleful little creature; first because I was alone; next because my Uncle James was ill and so could not be happy; and last because I was made to feel more homesick than ever by the cold glances and cold tongue of Miss Jemima."

"Miss Jemima!" echoed Susan, in her amusement, burying her face for an instant in her hands.

"Miss Jemima," repeated the old voice solemnly. "But I was not only dismal and doleful. Far worse: I made little attempt to be anything else, and began to be fretful too. There was no company of my own age, for, as you see, the village is a mile or two off—over there where the sun is lighting the trees up. And I was not allowed to play with the village children. The only company I had was a fat little boy of two, belonging to one of the farm hands. And he was so backward a baby, that even at that age he could scarcely say as many words."

"I began to talk at one," said Susan.

"Yes, my dear," said her grannie, "and you are likely, it seems, to go on talking the clock round."

"Grannie dear," said Susan, "I simply *love* this story—until—*you* know."

"Now of all the places where I was supposed not to go to," continued the old lady, "that churchyard was the very one. My aunt, as I say, thought me a fantastic, silly-notioned little girl, and she didn't approve of picking flowers that grow among tombstones. Indeed, I am not now quite sure myself if such flowers belong to the living at all. Still, once or twice in the summer the old sexton—Mr. Fletcher he was called, and a very grumpy old man he was—used to come with his scythe and mow the lush grasses down. And you could scarcely breathe for the sweet smell of them. It seemed a waste to see them lying in swaths, butterflies hovering above them, fading in the sun. There never were such buttercups and dandelion-clocks and meadow-sweet as grew beneath those old grey walls. I was happy there; and coming and going, I would say a prayer for my mother. But you will please understand, Susan, that I was being disobedient; that I had no business to be there at all—when I first came to know there was somebody else in the churchyard."

"Ah! somebody else," sighed Susan, sitting straight up, her eyes far away.

"It was one evening, rather like this one, but with a mackerel sky. The day before I had been stood in the corner for wearing an orange ribbon in my hair; and then sent to bed for talking to the grandfather's clock. I did it on purpose. And now—*this* evening, I was being scolded because I would not eat blackberry jam with my bread for tea. I was told it

was because I had been spoilt, and was a little town child who did not know that God had made the wild fruits for human use, and who thought that the only things fit to eat grew in gardens.

"Really and truly I disliked the blackberry jam because of the pips, and I had a hollow tooth. But I told my aunt that my mother didn't like blackberry jam either, which made her still more angry.

" 'Do you really think, James,' she said to my uncle, 'we should allow the child to grow up a dainty little minx like that? Now, see here, Miss, you will just stay there until you have eaten up the whole of that slice on your plate.'

" 'Well, then, Miss Jemima,' I said pertly, 'I shall stay here till I am eighty.'

" 'Hold your tongue,' she bawled at me, with eyes blazing.

" 'I can't bear the horrid——' I began again, and at that she gave me such a slap on my cheek that I overbalanced, and fell out of my chair. She lifted me up from the floor with a shake, set me in my chair again, and pushed it against the table till the edge was cutting into my legs. 'And now,' she said, 'sit there till you are eighty!'

"A look I had never seen before came into my uncle's face; his hands were trembling. Without another word to me, Miss Jemima helped him rise from his chair, and I was left alone.

"Never before had I been beaten like that. And I was almost as much frightened as I was hurt. I listened to the tall clock ticking, 'Wick-ed child, stub-born child,' and my tears splashed slowly down on the ugly slice of bread-and-jam on my plate. Then all of a sudden I clenched and shook my ridiculous little fist at the door by which she had gone out, wriggled back my chair, jumped out of it, rushed out of the house, and never stopped to breathe or to look back, until I found myself sitting huddled up under the biggest tomb in the churchyard; crying there, if not my heart out, at least a good deal of my sour little temper."

"Poor Grannie!" said Susan, squeezing her hand.

"There was not much 'poor' about that," was the reply.

"A pretty sight I must have looked, with my smeared face, green-stained frock and hair dangling. At last my silly sobbing ceased. The sky was flaming with the sunset. It was in June, and the air very mild and sweet. But instead of being penitent and realizing what a bad and foolish child I was, I began to be coldly rebellious. I stared at the rosy clouds and vowed to myself I'd give Miss Jemima a fright. I'd rather die than go back to the house that night. And when the thought of my mother came into my mind, I shut it out, saying to myself that she could not have cared how much I loved her, to leave me like this. And yet only a fortnight before a long letter had come to me from India!

"Well, there I sat. A snail came out of his day's hiding-place; moths began to appear; the afternoon's butterflies had all gone to rest. Far away I heard a hooting—and then a step. Cautiously peering up above my tombstone, I saw Maggie, one of the girls that helped on the farm. Her face was burning hot, and she was staring about her round the corner of the little church tower with her saucer blue eyes. She called to me, and at that my mouth opened and I made a shrill yelping squeal. She screeched too; her steel-tipped boot slipped on the flagstones; in an instant she was gone. And once more I was alone."

"Ah, but you weren't *really* alone, Grannie," whispered Susan, "were you?"

"That was just what I was going to tell you, my dear.

Immediately in front of my face stood some tall dandelion stalks, with their beautiful clocks, grey in the late evening light. And there were a few other gently nodding flowers. As I stared across them, on the other side of the flat grave-stone a face appeared. I mean it didn't rise up. It simply came into the air. A very small face, more oval than round, its gold-coloured hair over its wild greenish eyes falling on either side its head in a curious zigzag way—like this, I mean." The old lady took the hem of her skirt, and three or four times folded it together, then loosened it out.

"You mean, Grannie, as if it had been pleated," said Susan.

"Yes," said her grannie. "I noticed that most particularly. And very lovely it looked in the reddish light. The face was not smiling and did not appear to see me sitting there, no more than a lion does when he looks out of his cage at the people gathered round to see him fed. And yet I knew *she* knew that I was there. And though I did not think she minded my being there, I felt more frightened than I had ever been in my life. My mouth opened; I was clutching tight the grass on either side. And I saw nothing else as I stared into that tiny face."

"That was the Fairy, Grannie," said Susan, stooping forward again as if to make her words more impressive. The old lady glanced fixedly at the two blue eyes bent on her from under the brim of the round straw hat.

"At that moment, my dear, I did not know *what* it was. I was far too frightened to think. Time must have been passing, too, very quickly, for as I stared on, it was already beginning to be gloaming between us, and silent. Yes, much more silent even than this. Then, suddenly, behind me a low birdlike voice began to sing from out of the may-bushes, the notes falling like dewdrops in the air. I knew it was a nightingale. And at the very moment the thought came to me—That is a nightingale—the face on the other side of the rough grey stone vanished.

"For a few minutes I sat without moving—not daring to move. And then I ran, straight out of the churchyard by the way I had come, as fast as my legs could carry me. I hardly

know what I thought, but as soon as I saw the lights in the
upper windows of the farm, I ran even faster. Up under the
ilexes, and round through the farmyard to the back door. It
was unlatched. I slipped through, quiet as a mouse, into the
kitchen, climbed into the chair, and at once devoured every
scrap of that horrid bread-and-jam!

"And still, my dear, I don't believe I was really thinking,
only dreadfully afraid, and yet with a kind of triumph in my
heart that Miss Jemima should never know anything at all
about the face of the churchyard. It was all but dark in the
kitchen now, but I still sat on in my chair, even at last lifted
the plate, and insolently licked up with my tongue every
jammy crumb that was left.

"And then the door opened, and Miss Jemima stood there
in the entry with a lighted brass candlestick in her hand.
She looked at me, and I at her. 'Ah, I see you have thought
better of it,' she said. 'And high time too. You are to go
straight to bed.'

"If you can imagine, Susan, a cake made almost entirely
of plums, and every plum a black thought of hatred, I was
like that. But I said never a word. I got down from my chair,
marched past her down the flagstone passage, and she followed after. When I came to my uncle's door, I lifted my
hand towards the handle. 'Straight on, Miss,' said the voice
behind me. 'You have made him too ill and too unhappy to
wish you good-night.' Straight on I went, got into bed with

all my clothes on, even my dew-wet shoes, and stared at the ceiling till I fell asleep."

"You know, Grannie," said Susan, "it was very curious of you not even to undress at all. Why do you think you did that?"

"My dear," said her grannie, "at that moment I had such a hard, hot heart in me, that there was not any room for a why. But you see that little jutting attic window above the trees—it was in the room beyond that and on the other side of the house that I lay. And it's now seventy-five years ago. It may be there was even then a far-away notion in my mind of getting up in the middle of the night and running away. But whether or not, I was awakened by the sun streaming through my lattice window, for my bedroom lay full in the light of the morning.

"I could think of but one thing—my disgrace of the night before, and what I had seen in the churchyard. It was a dream, I thought to myself, shutting my eyes, yet knowing all the time that I did not believe what I was saying. Even when I was told at breakfast that my uncle was no better, I thought little of him, and gobbled down my porridge, with the one wish to be out of the house before I could be forbidden to go out. But the only sign of Miss Jemima was my dirty jam-stained plate of the night before, upon which she had put my hunch of breakfast bread. Yet although I was so anxious to get out, for some reason I chose very carefully

28

what I should wear, and changed the piece of ribbon in my hat from blue to green. A rare minx I was."

"You were, Grannie," said Susan, clasping her knees. "And then you went out to the churchyard again?"

"Yes. But all seemed as usual there; except only that a tiny bunch of coral-coloured berries lay on a flat leaf, on the very tombstone where I had hid. Now though I was a minx, my dear, I was also fairly sharp for my age, and after the first gulp of surprise, as I stood there among the nodding butter-cups, the sun already having stolen over the grey roof and shining upon the hot tombstones, I noticed a beady dew-drop resting on the leaf, and the leaf of as fresh a green as lettuce in a salad. Looking at this dewdrop I realized at once that the leaf could not have been there very long. Indeed, in a few minutes the sun had drunk up that one round drop of water, for it was some little time before I ventured to touch the berries.

"Then I knew in my heart I was not alone there, and that that green dish had been put there on purpose, just before I had come. The berries were lovely to look at, too; of a coral colour edging into rose. And I don't think it was because I had long ago been warned not to taste strange fruit, but be-cause I was uneasy in conscience already, that I did not nibble one then and there.

"It was very quiet in that green place, and on and on I watched, as still as a cat over a mouse's hole, though I myself really and truly was the mouse. And then, all of a sudden, flinging back my green dangling hat ribbon, I remember, over my shoulder, I said half-aloud, in an affected little voice, 'Well, it's very kind of you, I am sure,' stretched my hand across, plucked one of the berries, and put it into my mouth.

"Hardly had its juice tartened my tongue when a strange thing happened. It was as if a grasshopper was actually sitting in my hair, the noise of tiny laughter was so close. Besides this, a kind of heat began to creep into my cheek, and it seemed all the colours around me grew so bright that they dazzled my eyes. I closed them. I must have sat there for a while quite unconscious of time, for when I opened them again, the shadow had gone a pace or two back from the stone, and it was getting towards the middle of the morning.

"But there was still that dazzle in my eyes, and everything I looked at—the flowers and the birds, even the moss and lichen on the old stones, seemed as if they were showing me secrets about themselves that I had not known before. It seemed that I could share the very being of the butterfly that was hovering near; and could almost hear not only what the birds were singing, but what they were saying."

"Just like the fairy tales, Grannie."

"Yes," said the little old woman, "but the difference is that I was not happy about it. The flush was still in my cheek, and I could hear my heart beating under my frock,

and I was all of an excitement. But I knew in my inmost
self that I ought not to feel like that at all; that I had crept
into danger through my wicked temper; that those little un-
known coral fruits on the tombstone had been put there for
a trap. It was a bait, Susan; and I was the silly fish."

"O Grannie, a 'silly fish'!" said Susan. "I can see you
might feel wicked," she added, with a sage little nod, "but I
don't *exacaly* see why."

"That is just when it's most dangerous, my child," said her
grandmother, sharply closing her mouth very much indeed
like a fish. "But I must get on with my story, or we shall
never be home.

"I sat on, keeping my eyes as far as I could fixed on the invisible place in the air where I had seen the face appear, but nothing came, and gradually the scene lost its radiance, and the birds were chirping as usual again, and the butter-cups were the same as ever. No, not the same as ever, because, although it was a burning, sunny day, it seemed now that everything was darker and gloomier than usual on so bright a morning, and I skulked away home, feeling not only a little cold, but dejected and ashamed.

"As I went in through the gate between those two stone pillars you can just see by the round green tree down there, I looked up at the windows. And a dreadful pang seized me to see that their curtains were all drawn over the glass. And though I didn't know then what that meant, I knew it meant something sorrowful and tragic. Besides, they seemed like shut eyes, refusing to look at me. And when I went in, Miss Jemima told me that my uncle was dead. She told me, too, that he had asked to see me an hour or two before he died. 'He said, "Where is my little Susan?" And where you have been,' added Miss Jemima, 'is known only to your wicked wilful self.' I stared at her, and seemed to shrink until she appeared to be twice as large as usual. I could not speak, because my tongue would not move. And then I rushed past her and up the stairs into a corner between two cupboards, where I used sometimes to hide, and I don't know what I did or thought there; I simply sat on and on, with my hands clenched in my lap, everything I looked at all blurred, and my lips trying to say a prayer that would not come.

"From that day on I became a more and more wretched and miserable little girl, and, as I think now, a wickeder one. It all came of three things. First, because I hated Miss Jemima, and that is just like leaving a steel knife in vinegar, it so frets and wastes the heart. Next, because of the thought of my poor uncle speaking of me so gently and kindly when he was at death's door; and my remorse that I could never now ask him to forgive me. And last, because I longed to see again that magical face in the churchyard, and yet knew that it was forbidden."

"But, Grannie dear, you know," said Susan, "I never can see why you should have thought that then."

"No," replied the old lady. "But the point was, you see, that I *did* think it, and I knew in my heart that it would lead to no good. Miss Jemima made me go next day into the room where my uncle lay in his coffin. But try as she might to persuade and compel me, she could not make me open my eyes and look at him. For that disobedience she sent me to my bedroom for the rest of the day.

"When all was still, I crept out across the corridor into another room, and looked out over the trees towards the little church. And I said to myself, as if I were speaking to someone who would hear, 'I am coming to you soon, and no-body, *nobody* here shall ever see me again.'

"Think of it; a little girl not yet nine, angry with the whole world, and hardly giving a thought to the mother who was longing to see her, and—though I didn't know it then—was very soon to be in England again.

"Well, then came the funeral. I was dressed—I can see myself now, as I stood looking into the looking-glass—in a black frock trimmed with crape, with a tucker of white frilling round the neck, and an edging of it at the sleeves; my peaked white face and coal-black eyes.

"It was, as you see, but a very little distance to my poor uncle's last resting-place, and in those days they used a little hand-cart on wheels, which the men pushed in front of us, with its flowers. And Miss Jemima and I followed after it across the field. I listened to the prayers as closely as I could. But at last my attention began to wander, and, kneeling there beside Miss Jemima in the church, my hands pressed close to my eyes, for an instant I glanced out and up between my fingers.

"The great eastern window, though you cannot see it from here, is of centuries-old stained glass, crimson, blue, green. But in one corner, just above the narrow ledge of masonry outside, it had been broken many, many years ago by the falling of a branch of a tree, and had been mended with clear *white* glass. And there, looking steadily in and straight across and down at me, was the face and form of the being I had seen beside the tombstone.

34

"I cannot tell you, Susan, how beautiful that face looked then. Those rich colours of the saints and martyrs surrounding that gold hair—living gold—and the face as pale and beautiful—far more beautiful than anything else I had ever seen in my life before. But even then I saw, too, that into the morning church a kind of shadowy darkness had come, and the stone faces on either side the window, with their set stare, looked actually to be alive. I gazed between my fingers, hearing not a single word of what the old clergyman was saying, wondering when anyone else would see what I saw, and knowing that the smiling lips were breathing across at me, 'Come away, come away!'

"My bones were all cramped, and at last I managed to twist my head a little and peep up at Miss Jemima. The broad face beneath her veil had its eyes shut, and the lips were muttering. She had noticed nothing amiss. And when I looked again, the face at the window was vanished.

"It was a burning hot day—so hot that the flowers beside the grave were already withering before Miss Jemima took me home. We reached the stone porch together, and in its cold shadow she paused, staring down on me through her veil. 'You will be staying on here for a while, because I don't know what else to do with you,' she said to me. 'But you will understand that this is my house now. I am telling your mother how bad a child you are making yourself, and perhaps she will ask me to send you away to a school where they know how to deal with stubborn and ungrateful beings like yourself. But she will be sorry, I think, to hear that it was your wickedness that brought that poor kind body to its grave over there. And now, Miss, as the best part of the day is over, you shall have your bread-and-butter and milk in your bedroom, and think over what I have said.' "

"I think, Grannie," cried Susan, bending herself nearly double, "that that Miss Jemima was the most dreadful person I have ever heard of."

"Well, my dear," said her grandmother, "I have lived a good many years, and believe it is wiser to try and explain to oneself people as well as things. Do you suppose she would have been as harsh to me if I hadn't hated her? And now she lies there too, and I never had her forgiveness either."

Susan turned her head away and looked out over the countryside to the north, to where the roving horses had vanished, and where evening was already beginning gradually to settle itself towards night.

"And *did* you think over what Miss Jemima had said, Grannie?" she asked in a low voice.

"The first thing I did was to throw the bread-and-butter out of the window, and while I watched the birds wrangling over it and gobbling it up, I thought of nothing at all. It was cooler in the shade on that side of the house. My head ached after the sorrowful walk to the church and

back. I came away from the window, took off my black
frock, and sat there on the edge of my bed, I remember, in
my petticoat, not knowing what to do next. And then,
Susan, I made up my mind that I could not bear to be in
Miss Jemima's house for a day longer than I need.

"I was just clever enough to realize that if I wanted to
run away I must take care not to be brought back. I grew
hot all over at the thought of such a shame, never thinking
how weak and silly I was not to be able to endure patiently
what could only be a few more days or weeks before another letter came from my mother. Then I tore a leaf from
a book that was in my room—a Prayer Book—and scrawl-
ed a few words to my mother, saying how miserable *and*

wicked I had been, and how I longed to see her again. It's a curious thing, Susan, but I was pitying myself while I wrote those words, and thinking how grieved my mother would be when she read them, and how well Miss Jemima would deserve whatever my mother said to her. But I didn't utter a word in the letter about where I was going."

"You didn't really *know* where you were going, Grannie," whispered Susan, edging a little nearer. "Did you? Not *then,* I mean?"

"No, but I had a faint notion whom I was going *to;* for somehow, from old fairy tales I had got to believe that human children could be taken away to quite a different world from this—a country of enchantment. And I remembered having read, too, about two children that had come back from there, and had forgotten their own English."

"I know two poems about it," said Susan. "One about 'True Thomas'—'Thomas the Rhymer,' you know, Grannie, who stayed with the Queen of Fairyland for seven whole years, and another about . . . I do wonder—— But please, *please,* go on."

"Well, I hid my little letter in a cranny in the wainscot, after sewing a piece of cotton to it so that I might pull it out again when I wanted it. The next morning, I got up early, and slipping on my clothes, tiptoed out of the house before breakfast, and made my way to the church. I thought deceitfully that Miss Jemima would be sure to find out that I was gone, and that if for a morning or two she discovered me quietly sitting in the churchyard she would not suppose at another time, perhaps, that I was not safely there again. Plots, Susan, are tangled things, and are likely to tangle the maker of them too.

"The old man who took care of the church, Mr. Fletcher, to save himself the trouble of carrying the key of the door, used to hide it under a large stone beneath the belfry tower. I had watched him put it there. It was a fresh sparkling day, I remember, with one or two thin silver clouds high in the sky—angels, I used to call them—and I forgot for the moment in the brightness of it all my troubles, as I frisked along past the dewy hedges.

"My first thought was to make quite, quite sure about the Fairy Creature in the churchyard, my next to plan a way of escape. I gathered a bunch of daisies, and having come to the belfry door, I somehow managed to open it with the key which I dragged out from beneath its stone, and crept into the still, empty coolness. I had come to the conclusion, too, Susan, young though I was, that if the Fairy Creature or whatever she might be actually came into the church to me, it might be a proof there was no harm in her company, for I knew in my heart that I was in some mysterious danger.

"There are a few old oak pews in the little church, with

heads carved upon them, and one or two have side seats that draw out from the wood into the aisle. On one of these I sat down, so that while I could be intent on my daisy-chain— just to show I had something to do there—I could see out of the corner of my eye the open door by which I had come in. And I hadn't very long to wait.

"In the midst of the faint singing of the wild birds, out of the light that lay beyond the stone church wall I spied her come stealing. My heart almost stopped beating, nor did I turn my head one inch, so that my eyes soon ached because they were almost asquint with watching. If you can imagine a figure—even now I cannot tell you how tall she was—that seems to be made of the light of rainbows, and yet with every feature in its flaxen-framed face as clearly marked as a cherub's cut in stone; and if you can imagine a voice coming to you, close into your ear, without your being able to say exactly where it is coming *from— that* was what I saw and heard beneath that grey rood down there on that distant morning, seventy-five years ago. The longer I watched her out of the corner of my eye, the more certain I became that she was using every device she knew to attract my attention, even that she was impatient at my stupidity, and yet that she could not or did not dare to cross the threshold. And so I sat and watched her, fumbling on the while with my limpening daisy stalks. Many strange minutes must have passed like this.

"At last, however, having fancied I heard a footfall, I was surprised out of myself, and suddenly twisted my head. She too had heard, and was standing stiller than a shadow on snow, gazing in at me. I suppose thoughts reveal themselves in the face more swiftly than one imagines. I was partly afraid, partly longing to approach closer. I wished her to realize that I longed for her company, but that danger was near, for I was well aware whose step it was I had heard. And, as I looked at her, there came a sharpness into her face, a cold inhuman look—not of fear, but almost like hatred—and she was gone. More intent than ever, I stooped over my daisies. And in the hush there was a faint sound as of an intensely distant whistle.

"Then a shadow fell across the porch, and there was Miss Jemima. It's a strange thing, Susan, but Miss Jemima also did not enter the church. She called to me from where she stood, in almost a honeyed voice: 'Breakfast is ready, Susan.' "

"I can imagine *exacaly* how she said that, Grannie," said the little girl, "because my name's Susan, too."

"Yes, my dear," said the old lady, squeezing her hand. "It was passed on to you from me by your dear mother just because it was mine. And I hope you will always be the Susan I have *now*." From near at hand upon the hill a skylark suddenly took its flight into the evening blue. The old lady listened a moment before going on with her story.

"Well," she began again, "I gathered up my apron and walked towards Miss Jemima down the aisle. Suddenly there came a slight rumbling noise, which I could not understand. Then instantly there followed a crash. And at Miss Jemima's very feet, in the sunlight, I saw lying a piece of stone about the size of a small plum pudding. Miss Jemima gave a faint scream. Her cheek, already pale, went white; and she stared from me to the stone and back again, as I approached her.

" 'You were talking in there—in God's church—to someone,' she whispered harshly, stooping towards me. 'To whom?'

"I shook my head, and stood trembling and gazing at the stone.

" 'Look into my face, you wicked child,' she whispered. 'Who were you talking to in there?'

"I looked up at last. 'It's empty,' I said.

" 'There's a lying look in your eyes!' cried Miss Jemima. 'And you are the child that goes into a sacred place to weave daisy-chains! Turn you face away from me. Do you hear me, Miss? Miserable little *Sorceress* that you are!'

"The word seemed to flame up in my mind as if it had been written in fire on smoke; and still I stared at the stone. I felt but did not see Miss Jemima steadily turn her head and look around her.

" 'A few inches,' she added in a low voice, 'and you would have killed me.'

" 'Me!' I cried angrily. 'What has it to do with *me*, Miss Jemima?'

" 'Ah!' said she. 'We shall know a little more about that when you have told me what company you find here where your poor uncle might hope to be at rest.'

"It's a dreadful thing to confess, Susan, but up to that moment, though I had again and again cried by myself at memory of him, though tears were always in my heart for him, I hadn't thought of my uncle that morning.

" 'And perhaps,' added Miss Jemima, 'bread and water and solitude for a day or two will help to persuade your tongue.'

"I followed her without another word across the field, and in a few minutes was alone once more in my bedroom with a stale crust and glass of water to keep me company.

"I should think if my angry tears had run into the water that morning, they would have actually made it taste salt. But I cried so that not even a mouse could have heard me. Every other thought was now out of my mind—for I dared not even talk to myself about the stone—but that of getting away from the house forever. One thing I could not forget, however, and that was the word 'sorceress.' It terrified me far more than I can tell you. I knew in my young mind that Miss Jemima was treating me wickedly, however naughty I had been, and I knew too, in strange fear, that the stone might not have fallen by accident. I had seen the look on the

Fairy's face and . . . " The old lady suddenly broke off her story at this point, and looked about her in alarm. "My dear, we must go at once; the dew is beginning to fall, and the air is already colder."

"Oh, Grannie," said the child, "how I wish we might stay—a little, *little* longer!"

"Well, my dear, so do I. For I am old, and I shall never see this place again. It brings many memories back. Who knows what might have happened if——"

"But, Grannie," interrupted the child hastily, picking up the umbrella from the grass. "Please tell me the rest of the story straight, straight, straight on as we go back." It seemed to Susan, so still was her grandmother's face at that moment, and so absent her eyes—that she could not have heard her. The small aged eyes were once more looking carefully down on the scene below. For an instant they shut as if the old lady had thought so to remember it more completely. And then the two of them began slowly to climb the hill, and the story proceeded.

"No one disturbed me during the long morning," continued the old voice, "but in the afternoon the door was unlocked, and Miss Jemima opened it to show in the Reverend Mr. Wilmot, who conducted the service in the church every other Sunday. I won't tell you all he said to me. He was a kind and gentle old man, but he didn't so much as think it possible there was any being or thing in the churchyard but

its birds, its tombstones, and now and then a straying animal. He only smiled about all that, nor did he ask me Miss Jemima's question.

"He took my hand in his great bony one and begged me to be a good little girl. And I see his smiling face as he asked it. 'Not only for your mother's sake,' he said, 'but *for goodness' sake.*'

"'I am sure, my dear,' he went on, 'Miss Jemima *means* to be kind, and all *we* have to do is to mean to be good.'

"I gulped down the lump in my throat, and said, 'But don't you think *sorceress* is a very wicked word?'

"He stood up, holding both my hands in his. 'But my poor little lamb,' he cried, 'Miss Jemima is no more a sorceress than I am a Double Dutchman!' And with that he stooped, kissed the top of my head, and went out of the room.

"In a minute or two his footsteps returned. He opened the door an inch and peeped in. 'Why, we are better already!' he smiled at me over his spectacles. Then he came in, carrying a plate with a slice of bread-and-jam upon it, and a mug of milk. 'There,' he said, 'there's no sorcery in that, is there? And now you will be an obedient and gentle child, and think how happy Mamma will be to see you.'"

"I think," said Susan stoutly, "that that Mr. Wilmot is one of the kindest men I ever knew."

Her grandmother looked down on her with a crooked smile on her face. "He was so kind, Susan, that I never mentioned to him that the blackberry-jam on the bread was not a great favorite of mine! A moment after the sound of his steps had died away I heard the key once more in the lock. And what did I say to myself when he was gone? I looked

forlornly at the plate, then out of the window, and I believe, Susan, that I did what they sometimes describe in the story-books—I wrung my hands a little, repeating to myself, *'He doesn't understand. No! He doesn't understand.'*

"In an hour or two, Miss Jemima herself opened the door and looked in. She surveyed me where I sat, and then her glance fell on the untouched slice of bread-and-jam.

" 'Ah,' said she, 'a good man like Mr. Wilmot cannot realize the hardness of a stubborn heart. I don't want to be unkind to you, Susan, but I have a duty to perform to your mother and to your poor uncle. You shall not leave this room until you apologize to me for your insolence of this morning, and until you tell me whom you were speaking to in the church.'

"The lie that came into my mind—'But I was not speaking to anyone, Miss Jemima'—faded away on my tongue. And I simply looked at her in silence.

" 'You have a brazen face, Susan,' said she, 'and if you grow up as you are now, you will be a very wicked woman.' "

"I think," said Susan, *"that* was a perfectly dreadful thing to say, Grannie."

"Times change, my dear," said the old lady. "And now—well, it is fortunate that there is very little more to tell. For this hill has taken nearly all the breath out of my body!"

The two of them were now on the crest of the hill. The light was beginning to die away in the sky, and the mists to grow milkier in the hollows of the flat country that lay around and beneath them. Far, far away, facing them across the wild, a reddish-coloured moon was rising. From low down below, a dog barked—it might be from dead Miss Jemima's farmyard. The little church surrounded by its low wall seemed to have gathered in closer to its scattered stones.

"Yes, Grannie dear?" breathed Susan, slipping her hand into the cotton-gloved one that hung near. "What then?"

"Then," replied her grandmother, "the door was locked again. Anger and hatred filled that silly little body sitting in the bedroom, and towards evening I fell asleep. And I must have dreamed a terrifying dream, though when I awoke I could not remember my dream—only its horror. I was terrified at it in that solitude, and I knew by the darkening at the window that it must be at least nine or ten o'clock. Night was coming, then. I could scarcely breathe at the thought. A second mug of milk had been put beside the plate; but I could not even persuade myself to drink any of it.

"Then in a while I heard Miss Jemima's footsteps pass my room. She made no pause there, and presently after I knew that she was gone to bed. She had not even troubled to look in on her wretched little prisoner. The hardness of that decided me.

"I tiptoed over to the door, and with both hands softly twisted the handle. It was still locked. Then I went to the window and discovered, as if the Fairy Creature herself had

50

magicked it there, that a large hay-wain half full of hay, its shafts high in the air, had been left drawn up within a few feet of my window. It looked dangerous, but it was not actually a very difficult jump even for a child of my age; and I think I might have jumped even if there had been no cart at all. My one thought was to run away. *Anywhere*—so long as there was no chance of Miss Jemima's finding me.

"But even in that excited foolish moment I had sense enough left—before I jumped out of the window—to take a little warm jacket out of my chest-of-drawers, and to wrap my money-box up in a scarf so that it should not jangle too much. I pulled my letter up from its cranny in the wainscot by its thread, and put it on the pink dressing table. And at that moment, in the half-dark I saw my face in the looking-glass. I should hardly have recognized it. It looked nearly as old, Susan, as I do now."

"Yes, dear Grannie," said Susan.

"Then I jumped—without the slightest harm to myself. I scrambled down into the yard and, keeping close to the house, crept past the kennel, the old sheep dog merely shaking her chain with her thumping tail a little as I passed. And then, as soon as I was beyond the tall gateposts, I ran as fast as my legs would carry me."

"But *not*," cried Susan almost with a shout in the still air, "*not* to the churchyard, Grannie. I think that was the most wonderful thing of all."

"Not so very wonderful, my dear, if you remember that I was now intensely afraid of the Fairy Creature, after seeing that look in her countenance when Miss Jemima was approaching the church. Something in me had all along, as you know, said, *Don't be deceived by her. She means you no well.* I cannot explain that; but so it was. Yet all the time I had been longing to follow where she might lead. Why she should wish to carry off a human child I don't know, but that she really wanted me I soon discovered for certain.

"If you follow the tip of my umbrella, you will just be able to see, Susan, a large meadow on the other side of the farm. But I don't think even your sharp eyes will detect the stones standing up in it. They are called the Dancers, and though I was a little frightened of passing them in the darkness, this was the only way to take. Gradually I approached them, my heart beating beneath my ribs like a drum, until I was come near.

"And there, lovelier than ever, shining as fairly as if with a light of her own, sitting beneath the largest of the Dancers, directly in my path, was She. But this time I knew she was not alone. I cannot describe what passed in my heart. Still I longed to go, still I was in anguish at the thought of it. I didn't dare to look at her, and all I could think to do was to pretend not to see anything. How I had the courage I cannot think. Perhaps it was the courage that comes when fear and terror are almost beyond bearing.

"I put my money-box on to the grass; the scarf was already wet with dew. Then, very slowly, I put my black jacket on and buttoned it up. And then, with face turned away from the stone, I walked slowly on down the path, between the Dancers, towards the one that is called the Fiddler, in their midst. The night air was utterly silent. But as I approached the stone, it seemed as if it were full of voices and footsteps and sounds of wings and instruments, yet all as small as the voices of grasshoppers.

"I just kept saying, 'Oh, please, God; oh, please, God,' and walked on. And when at last I came to the stone, the whole world suddenly seemed to turn dark and cold and dead. Apart from the ancient stone, leaning up out of the green turf as it had done for centuries, there was not a sign or a symptom, Susan, of anything or anybody there."

"I think I can *just* see the stone, Grannie, but I would not be there like that in the dark, not for anything—anything in the world. . . . I expect it was what you *said* made the Fairy go. And then, Grannie?"

"Then, Susan, my heart seemed to go out of me. I ran on, stumbling blindly for a little way, then lost my balance completely over a tussock of grass or a mole-heap and fell flat on my face. Without any words that I can remember, I lay praying in the grass.

"But even then I did not turn back. I got up at last and ran on more lightly, and without looking behind me, across the field. Its gate leads into a by-road. It was padlocked, and as I mounted to the top my eyes could see just above a slight rise in the ground, for the lane lies beneath a little hill there.

"And coming along the road towards me there were shining the lamps of a carriage. I clambered down and crouched in the hedge-side, and in a few moments the lamps re-appeared at the top of the incline and the horse came plod-plodding along down the hill. It was a wonderful mild summer night, the sky all faint with stars. What would have happened if it had been cold or pouring with rain I cannot think. But because it was so warm, the air almost like milk, the hood of the carriage was down.

"And as it came wheeling round by the hedge-side, I saw

in the filmy starlight who it was who was sitting there. Neither horse nor coachman could see me. I jumped to my feet and ran after the carriage as fast as my legs could carry me, screaming at the top of my voice, 'Mother, Mother!'

"Perhaps the grinding of the wheels in the flinty dust and the noise of the hoofs drowned my calling. But I still held tight to my money-box, and though it was muffled by the scarf in which it was wrapped, at each step it made a dull noise like a bird-scare, and this must at last have attracted my mother's attention. She turned her head, opened her mouth wide at sight of me—I see her now—then instantly jumped up and pulled the coachman's buttoned coat-tails. The carriage came to a standstill. . . .

"And that," said the old lady, turning away her head for one last glance of the countryside around her, "that is all, Susan."

Susan gave a last great sigh. "I can't think what you must have felt, Grannie," she said, "when you were safe in the carriage. And I can't——" But at this point she began to laugh very softly to herself, and suddenly stood still. "And I can't think either," she went on, "what Miss Jemima must have thought when you and *Great*-Grannie knocked at the door. You did tell me once that she opened her bedroom window at the sound of the knocking, and looked out in her nightdress. I expect she was almost as frightened as you were among those Dancers."

The two of them were now descending the hill on the side away from the farm and the church. And not only their carriage standing beneath them, but the evening star had come into view. There never was such a peaceful scene —the silver birches around them standing perfectly still, clothed with their little leaves, and the rabbits at play among the gorse and juniper.

"Bless me, Mum," said the old cabman as he opened the carriage door, "I was just beginning to think them fairises had runned away with you and the young lady."

Susan burst completely out laughing. "Now don't you think, Grannie," she said, "that is a very, very curious quincidence?"